Rethinking Church

9 STRATEGIES TO ENGAGE CONGREGATIONS AND COMMUNITIES IN MINISTRY

LaKesha Womack

Contents

Getting started…

I'm LaKesha Womack and at the time of this workbook's first publication, I have 15 years of experience working with churches, business owners, not for profit organizations, corporations, and colleges/universities. I specialize in creating strategies for personal and organizational growth.

I am also the published author of 14 additional books with more than 40 pieces of business advice listed on Forbes.com. As I gain knowledge in an area, I seek ways to share that information with others because I truly believe that knowledge is power and we should all strive to become powerful.

This workbook is designed for congregations seeking ideas for strategic growth. There are nine categories to assess and they are by no means the totality of what should be considered when creating a church growth strategy but they are a starting point. As you work with your group, you may find other areas that need to be addressed. There is a page included for you to list those as notes. And by all means, write in this book, make notes, scratch things out, highlight… make it work for you!

Format – each section will begin with some ideas for you to consider as you are rethinking how to "do" church. From there, you can brainstorm on your strengths and weakness (internal)/ opportunities and threats (external). Then, you will need to create action items. What can you do immediately (within the next six months), short term (within the next year), and long term (within 3-5 years) to achieve the goal?

Think SMART! Are the goals: specific, measurable, action-oriented, realistic, and time-specific?

In the wrap-up, you will choose one project from each section to begin working on. As you complete that project, add another from your list and keep going until you no longer need this list and your church is engaging in impact ministry that connects your congregation and community.

Caution: This workbook is not going to walk you through the academic research and causes of church decline. Feel free to do your research to find those statistics. I am also not going to quote scripture to convince you that God wants your church to grow. You should know that. I am focused on helping you to develop practical strategies that will work for your congregation.

Note to self

What do I hope will change in my church as a result of working through this book? What are some of our strengths and weaknesses? What are some opportunities and threats that can prevent us from growing?

Strengths – what are we doing well?	Weaknesses – what can we do better?
1 2 3	1 2 3
Opportunities – who can help us?	Threats – what can stop us?
1 2 3	1 2 3

Rethinking Church

Many traditional churches have failed to recognize the changes in the models of ministry in the United States and have been suffering from a decline in ministry and engagement as a result. We can examine a multitude of factors that have contributed to this decline and cite numerous sources to understand it's causes but my time with you will be better spent looking forward. When trying to understand how the traditional black church went from being the center of the black community to now having communities consider whether the church is necessary; the cause can be simplified – a refusal to change. Churches that have failed to closely monitor the changes around them and make adjustments to ensure they are relevant are now struggling to keep their doors open. Churches that have failed to create disciples through spiritual formation are now struggling with the faithful few doing most of the work while the majority of the members are nowhere to be seen. Churches that have not developed ministries that meet the needs of the congregations and communities are struggling to understand why people are not showing up for their revivals and programs.

Just as every other industry in our country has changed in the past 50 years, so too must the church change. The message of Jesus Christ as our Risen Savior does not change but the methods used to share that message must be relevant to the persons the church intends to serve. Those methods will be different for every congregation. No one fix will save every church but each church must do a serious self-examination to examine why they are not growing, do they really want to grow, and how much are they willing to invest in the growth. Most importantly, there must be an understanding of church growth because it is not always a numerical pursuit. We often miss the mark when attempting to fill our pews with large numbers of people rather than focusing on the spiritual growth of the few in our midst.

As society began to embrace technology as a means of social communication and business efficiency, the church did not identify how this would impact ministry. Although there have been moves towards creating Facebook pages to connect with members and visitors, posting photos and flyers on Instagram, adding sermon snippets to Twitter, creating website designs to rank higher in search engine results, and streaming worship experiences; very few churches have developed a strategic plan to engage in ministry that meets the needs of its members and visitors while using technology and social media as a tool for engagement.

Additionally, many churches have not embraced small group discipleship as a means of creating relationships with God and with members within their congregations. The failure to properly disciple new members often results in a revolving door of members. Rather than becoming connected with the ministries of the church and finding ways to serve, members are joining and leaving for other options. This is evident when analyzing the number of members on a roll in contrast with the number of persons who regularly attend worship and/or participate in ministry. When taking a closer examination of the class leader or small group leader system, many of the group leaders are doing random check-ins or making contact when there is a financial need. This type of communication does not aid in the spiritual growth of the members which can be one of the reasons that they continue searching for a spiritual home. Many other factors contribute to members not regularly contributing to the church community; however, an effective utilization of the class leader system is a tool to increase the probability of engagement.

Finally, taking a critical examination of our ministries and who they serve will assist in not only attracting visitors but also in engaging existing members. Many congregations would experience exponential growth if they were able to effectively connect with the people who have already said "yes" to their church. Those people are your most likely cheerleaders and can be the catalyst for your resurgence. When their spiritual and physical needs are being met, they are more likely to invite others to partake in what they are experiencing. In many instances, we bring in new people but don't cultivate the relationship with them and instead go out searching for more new people to bring in. Shifting our thinking to relationship building with existing members will also create more sustainable growth.

Rethinking how we "do" church requires an examination of our church culture. Although many churches aspire for growth, they are often resistant to change. Nothing grows without change; therefore, it is necessary to identify what the church is doing well but also to seriously examine areas for improvement. Through this workbook, you can assess the strengths and weaknesses within your congregation as well as the opportunities and threats within your community to create a plan for your church's growth.

I would like to challenge you to set God-size goals for your long-term goals. These are goals that can only be attained if God is truly in the midst of your work. Pray to discern what God would want for your church and for your community and begin the work through your immediate and short-term goals to achieve it. Just as our grandparents stepped out on faith to build structures that many of us still worship in today, we can step out on faith to create ministries that our future generations will benefit from.

Exercise:
Assess the strengths and weaknesses within your church when dealing with change. How has your church changed in the past five years? Ten years? Twenty years? Where do you see the church in the next five years? Ten years? Twenty years?

Does your leadership have a "we've always done it this way attitude" or a "let's try and see what happens" culture?

Are your members ready for growth? Does the culture of the church embrace new people? Not only as visitors but is space made for them in the leadership and participation of ministries?

Rethinking Church

Goal:

STRENGTHS	WEAKNESSES

Action Items

Immediate (within 6 months)

Short Term (within one year)

Long Term (within 3-5 years)

Notes:

Discipleship Training for Leaders

If we can be honest, many churches have placed more focus on creating members than creating disciples. I do not believe this was done intentionally; however, we cannot neglect the detrimental effect that it has had on the church. We have mistakenly confused salvation – accepting Jesus Christ as our Lord and Savior – with discipleship – following the teachings of Jesus and teaching others.

I often wondered why more people did not boldly profess their faith as a tool for church recruiting. It seemed that if we have such a good thing with Christ and our lives have been changed then we should want to offer that gift to everyone. After some examination, I realized that many churches provide opportunities for the study of scripture but there are not always opportunities for members, especially new members, to wrestle with their faith so that they gain a true understanding of how salvation has and is playing a role in their spiritual walk. It almost seems that after a person becomes a member, we expect divine knowledge to be imparted into them and for them to become a mature Christian.

However, it is our job to not only bring new people into the family of faith but to also walk with them as they grow into mature Christians so that they can then walk with others. Ideally, this process should be done through your class leader system on an ongoing basis. This does not have to replace your New Member's Classes and Orientations but we have to be cognizant that people mature at different rates. Small group leaders should be prepared to walk with the members of their small group as long as it takes for them to develop to a level where they can ultimately lead their own small group. Many of the class leader models that I have seen are more tribal with no goals for the independence of the members or plans for them to grow beyond where they are currently.

Imagine with me for a moment... a church has 50 members with five class leaders. Each class leader has ten members but only four to six members in each class is active. The class leader calls occasionally to check on the members and to ensure they remain in good standing (whatever that means in your context). Some of the members are responsive while others feel like the class leader is only calling when they want something. The pastor has noticed this disturbing trend and identifies resources for the discipleship training of her class leaders. Through the training, the class leaders are taught principles for the spiritual formation and development of their class members. They decide to contact their class members weekly to engage in spiritual conversations with their members. As the relationships among the leaders and members continue to develop, the members begin to identify their spiritual gifts and their calling. They begin to participate in the ministries of the church, first receiving services and training then moving to serve others. They are introduced to the idea of creating a small group of their own among some new members from the church and some of their friends. Excited about their own spiritual growth, they are hesitant but with the discipleship training, they are willing to try it.

Although this is an idealized situation, can you see how this process would create a more engaged leadership and more members participating and growing in ministry? Our goal should not be to get members to join our churches but to get people to accept Christ, to become disciples and to disciple others. During that process, we offer programs and provide ministries to meet their physical needs while working toward spiritual growth. In so many instances, we are doing one or the other. We are offering great programs and ministries but we are not helping the individual with their personal walk or we have the spiritual development but people are still seeking services to meet their physical needs.

Exercise:

What are the strengths and weaknesses of your church's discipleship training? How can it be improved to create more engagement?

What resources are you using for discipleship training? Is the training producing the desired results? How often is the training provided? Are the leaders using the tools?

Discipleship Training

Goal:

STRENGTHS	WEAKNESSES

Action Items

Immediate (within 6 months)

Short Term (within one year)

Long Term (within 3-5 years)

Notes:

Evaluation of Class Leader System

In the previous section, we discussed the benefits of discipleship training so that class leaders can emphasize the spiritual formation of their class members. If your church is to grow, small group systems are one of the keys to your growth.

People can watch sermons from anywhere on their smartphones, televisions, tablets in lieu of your Sunday morning sermon. They can study the Bible daily through mobile applications in lieu of your bible study. They can volunteer with numerous not for profit organizations to serve their community in lieu of participating in your ministries. What can set your church apart is not preaching, the choir, the programs or even the building. People will forsake all of that for genuine relationships.

According to Maslow's Hierarchy of Needs (see Appendix), after having our psychological and safety needs met; we want to be loved and to belong. Our psychological needs are considered air, water, food, shelter, clothing, and reproduction. Those are what many consider to be our basic needs. Our safety needs are considered to be personal security, employment, resources, health, and property. Many ministries attempt to satisfy some of the elements within those first two levels however we often miss reaching the third level – love and belonging.

Even if we are doing a great job with providing programs and ministries that meet the needs of our congregation and community, the culture of our church will have an impact on whether they feel as if they belong. Class leaders can be extremely helpful in facilitating this process. Not only could they contact members to walk with them along their spiritual journey but they can also plan group activities to help the members build relationships with one another, assess the spiritual gifts of the members to ensure they are paired with ministry opportunities that fit their gifts, and ensure they feel welcome when they come to church. Imagine how this type of relationship-building would create a connection for the members – not only the new members but also some of the existing members that you are trying to encourage to come back or to stay. We can not dismiss the importance of creating a loving environment within the church.

Church hurt is real and too often we allow members who have a negative disposition to chase away members. If you know that there are people who are causing this type of harm within the church; it must be dealt with lovingly. Do not allow a few people to impede the growth of your church. The energy can be felt when you enter the church and certain people aren't talking to others or when you sit in the wrong seat and are promptly chastised for not understanding the invisible assigned seating chart. If this energy exists within your church, work on it before you begin to implement strategies to engage the community. You don't want to turn them off from the prospect of joining your community.

Class leaders should be the ambassadors of the church. Some churches have assigned a class leader to the visitors. They are in charge of making contact with the visitor and periodically following up with them to see if they have found a church home. Because so many churches have a revolving door mentality, this direct connection is very powerful to people are seeking a genuine connection with a congregation.

Exercise:
Evaluate your class leader system. What are you doing well? What are some areas for improvement?

Class Leaders

Goal:

STRENGTHS	WEAKNESSES

Action Items

Immediate (within 6 months)

Short Term (within one year)

Long Term (within 3-5 years)

Notes:

Analysis of Congregational Demographics

Meeting the needs of the persons within your congregation should be a priority. Take a moment to assess the demographics of the persons who are already members of your church to begin identifying ministries to focus on. When you are meeting their needs, they will begin to invite others who are like them to attend. If your members are not inviting others to attend worship, bible study or your programs, it is probably because they do not believe others will enjoy it or find value. We are a social culture. When we like something, we want to share it.

Age Groups – children (newborn – 12), youth (12-21), young adults (22-40), adults (41-65), mature adults (66+)

A healthy church should have a mix of all age groups in their congregation. Is there one group that you have a larger number of members? Ensure that you have ministries in place that meet their needs so they don't feel neglected before moving toward meeting the needs of persons that you want to attract. For example, if you have a healthy mix of children and youth, what evening and weekend activities are you planning to keep them engaged with the church and with each other. If you have young adults, consider some of the life skills they may need help developing and workshops that may be appealing to them and their friends. Don't neglect the needs of your adults who often end up being the workers of the church. What are their needs and what ministries can be offered to provide resources for them? Most importantly, consider ministries for your mature adults such as day activities, home clean-up and repair assistance, and outings. Knowing who you have will help to determine where to start.

What is the ratio of men to women?

Many churches have more women than men in their congregations and seem to be confused as to why. Take a look at the programs and ministries that you are offering. Are any of them speaking to the spiritual needs of men? Men are more than handymen in the church. Ensure you are planning activities that speak to their spiritual as well as social needs.

Which schools are your children and youth attending?

It is disheartening to hear the amount of out of pocket resources teachers are spending on their classrooms. Can you imagine the look on your children and youth member's faces if their church adopted their classroom? Adopting a classroom is a great idea but being intentional and adopting the classrooms of your members will create a sense of pride within those students who can become your biggest cheerleaders. Send members to read to their classes, volunteer when needed and build relationships with the students and teachers.

Where do your members work?

How many years have you seen members in your church and had no idea where they worked? Some people have worked jobs for years and retired with few people having any idea of what they do professionally. Your members can be your greatest resources for workshop presenters, event sponsors, and economic empowerment drivers. When your class leaders assess the spiritual gifts of their members and know what they do professionally, seek ways to support them. Ask the attorney to host a legal workshop. Ask the congregation to support a small business of the month. Too often the church asks for support from the members while failing to seek ways to support its members, aside from those whose skills might be used on steward and trustee boards. Think more broadly about how you can support your members and help them to build their business and professional resume.

What is the relationship status of your members (single, divorced, married, widowed)?

Creating ministries around the relationship status of members is not meant to be a matchmaking service but an opportunity for groups of people in similar life stages to develop relationships with one another. For example, your singles ministry might want to start a restaurant club while the married ministry might want to plan a retreat. Having a divorced ministry in place may help you to retain members who are going through a divorce because they will have a place to process their feelings in a supportive environment. A grief ministry, not only for widows but anyone dealing with loss, is a great opportunity to help people who have lost a loved one. We often show up at the funeral and repass but there are not often ongoing support services to help people not only deal with the void of losing their loved one but this is often a time when people begin to question God's decision to take their loved one and their personal relationship with Him.

What are the interests of your members?

For many people, Christianity is not only a two-day activity but they attempt to live their faith throughout the week. What are some ways that you can engage them outside of the church? Is there a bowling alley with a bowling league that a group can sign up for? Do you have any golfers who might want to play with each other? Are there foodies who might want to try new restaurants once per month? Any movie fanatics who enjoy seeing new movies when they come out? What about your kids? What do they enjoy doing? How can you plan activities around what they enjoy so that they don't view Christianity as only something they do in the church?

Exercise:

Each class leader should have this information about their members (age, gender, relationship status, school/employment, etc.). Work with your class leaders to begin discussing which ministries can be developed that will be of interest to the people who are already members of the congregation. You want to have a mix of educational opportunities like seminars and workshops but also plan social events like dinner and movie outings so that the members can develop relationships with each other. Also, make sure they know that it is ok to invite others to participate. The more the merrier!

Tip: start small and be consistent. When you start these ministries, only a few people will show up and participate. Do not despise small beginnings. Use these events to get to know your attendees and find out what they think can be done to make the events better. Take the advice and use it for future planning. Seek to always improve and do not get discouraged. At the end of each event, you should already have the next event planned and be prepared to share those details so that you can keep your members and attendees looking forward to what's next.

Congregational Demographics

Goal:

STRENGTHS	WEAKNESSES

Action Items

Immediate (within 6 months)

Short Term (within one year)

Long Term (within 3-5 years)

Notes:

Invest in Infrastructure

Many older churches do have the resources to remodel and create a modern structure. However (!!!), every church can be clean and decluttered. Although it can be tempting to want to decorate your church, consider a minimalist approach. This may seem confusing but consider this… a person who is new to "church" comes in and you have stuff everywhere – signs, flags, banners, plants, old equipment, broken furniture – what do you think they are going to be paying more attention to? All of your stuff or the worship experience? Everything in your sanctuary should contribute to the worship experience.

Having signs strategically placed that identify the liturgical season or that are affirmations of our faith are great but don't go overboard and make sure they are clean and well maintained. Having plants and flowers are beautiful but make sure they are well cared for and the potters are clean. If there are items that are broken and no longer being used, remove them to free up space. Many churches are amazed at how liberating it feels to declutter and clean their church. Your church should not look like nor be the member's junkyard. Don't allow people to "donate" items to the church that they don't want in their homes. If it is not going to serve a purpose in the church, take it to Goodwill.

Exercise:

Start at the driveway of the church and begin looking at your church like a first-time visitor. Many times we overlook things because we are accustomed to seeing them. What do you see without context (understanding the reason it was put there)?

- Driveway – when people first pull into the parking area of your church

- Yard – how well is the exterior landscape maintained
- Signage – can it be viewed easily
- Building – are there any repairs that need to be made to the external structure
- Entrance – is it free of clutter, clean, inviting; is it wheelchair accessible
- Bathrooms – are they clean, well-stocked and fresh smelling
- Sanctuary – are the elements contributing to or distracting from worship, it is well lit, is the temperature appropriate for the season
- Classrooms – are they clean and able to be used by organizations other than the church
- Fellowship Hall – is it clean and able to be used by organizations other than the church

As you are doing your walkthrough, make a list of things that need to be improved but don't forget to highlight the areas that are appealing. Based on your list, you can start to prioritize the work that needs to be done. As your membership starts to increase, begin using a portion of the funds to make these improvements. It will be exciting for the members to see their resources being used toward reinvigorating the infrastructure.

Side Note: if your church does not have any infrastructure needs, ask someone who is not a member to do the walkthrough for confirmation

Infrastructure

Goal:

STRENGTHS	WEAKNESSES

Action Items

Immediate (within 6 months)

Short Term (within one year)

Long Term (within 3-5 years)

Notes:

Evangelize Local Community

Once you have done the work inside you can begin to engage those outside of the church to invite them in. Too often, we want to bring new people into spaces that are not ready for them. This is like inviting someone to your home in the middle of an argument, before you've cleaned, or when there is no space for them to get comfortable. We must be intentional about creating a comfortable and loving culture for the community.

To get started, you need the demographics within a one-mile, five-mile and ten-mile radius of the church. Who are your neighbors? What is their race, age, median income? This information will be useful before you make contact because you need to know who you are talking to.

Next, identify which of the established ministries will appeal to your neighbors and which ministries you might consider establishing. Create a high-quality one-page information sheet that not only outlines your worship, Sunday School, and Bible Study times but also some of the programs that you offer and ministries available.

Then, provide an evangelism training for members who are interested in going out to greet the community. This can include knocking on doors, hosting a community BBQ in the church parking lot, setting up a booth at a local festival, and any other opportunities to share information about the church. This training is necessary because you will undoubtedly encounter people who do not believe in God, who have been hurt by the church, who have questions about their faith, who want to be prayed for, and who have a multitude of other issues. Training persons who are interested in this type of ministry will give them the confidence to engage in conversation rather than just putting materials in people's hands. The point is not to give your one sheet to as many people as possible but to create a relationship with as many people as possible so that they feel a connection with someone at the church. You want the invitation to come from someone sincere about beginning a spiritual journey with new people.

Make the ask. You want to ask them for something that won't cost them anything. If you are knocking on doors, consider letting them know that you are from the church and the church is starting new ministries and would like to know what ministries they would be interested in. If you are at a community event, ask them to complete a one question comment card in exchange for a bottle of water and a snack. At a community event at the church, you might want to have a one question comment card in exchange for giveaways. Keep in mind that the comment cards are optional. If people want the giveaway without completing the comment card, give them the item. Don't create negative "press" over something that you're planning to give away anyway.

Finally, follow up. After you have collected their information and given them information about the church follow up. You should have an email address to add to your email marketing list under prospects or a mailing address to send quarterly postcards. Encourage the evangelists to also follow up with a phone call.

Exercise:
Assess what you are currently doing to engage your local community. What are you doing well? What can you do better?

Evangelism

Goal:

OPPORTUNITIES	THREATS

Action Items

Immediate (within 6 months)
Short Term (within one year)
Long Term (within 3-5 years)

Notes:

Partner with Community Organizations

You don't have to do the work of ministry alone. There are probably organizations and not for profits who are already serving your community. Many of them are suffering from a lack of funding and a lack of volunteers. Once you identify the needs within your congregation and community that you want to meet, determine which organizations are providing the services and are interested in partnerships. This does not have to be a formal, contractual agreement rather a commitment to support organizations whose missions and visions align with the church.

You can partner in several ways – promote their services to your members, ask members to volunteer to help the organization, donate requested materials, donate money, and/or allow them to use space at the church at little to no charge (remember when focused on cleaning and decluttering the fellowship hall and classrooms). Opening your church to your partners not only allows the community to begin seeing the church as an extension of their services but it also brings in new people who may not have otherwise thought to enter your facility. If you are a smaller congregation, this strategy is also useful in helping you to have a greater impact in the community without exhausting your manpower.

If there are colleges or universities within close proximity of your church, this is another opportunity for partnership. Rather than waiting for the students to come to the church, consider partnering with a group like the black student union to host a bible study for their members, to sponsor a meal at one of their meetings, to provide mentorship opportunities, and to offer rides to the church on Sundays. (Note: don't forget about your members who are college students. Make sure you are sending them regular communications and care packages so that they remain connected to the church, even if they don't return after college. The goal is to maintain the relationship.)

Finally, avoid toxic charity. Many ministries unintentionally create a state of dependency through their ministries because they fail to help people deal with the underlying issues that have created the manifested problem. For example, if you have a food pantry and you have 100 people coming and the number continues to rise with the same people and new people then you are not addressing the issue. The goal should be fewer people needing your service or an increase in participation with new people. To accomplish this, it will be necessary to do some type of intake questioning to determine how the need developed and to begin developing a plan of action to meet that need. If participants are seeking employment then setting up computers to help them with a job search or having a list of companies that are hiring can be beneficial. If the issue is budgeting or they ran out of money before the end of their cycle, providing recipes that will help them make their food shopping budget go further or providing assistance with applying for food benefits can be beneficial.

Returning to Maslow's Hierarchy of Needs, the ultimate goal is self-actualization, helping people to become the best that they can be. It is not to create a dependency on the ministries. When we help people to begin the process of becoming whole, healthy, and happy; they are able to begin helping others.

Exercise:
What organizations can you partner with in your community? What services are they providing that will be beneficial to your members? What can you do to help them? How are you partnering with local youth and college organizations? How can you avoid practicing toxic charity?

Partnerships

Goal:

OPPORTUNITIES	THREATS

Action Items

Immediate (within 6 months)

Short Term (within one year)

Long Term (within 3-5 years)

Notes:

Build Relationships with Local Elected Officials

Most cities have a 20 or 50 strategic plan for their development and each year they are systematically executing portions of that plan. The communities around most of our churches have been slowly changing over the past 20, 10 or five years. These changes are not by happenstance and hopefully, you have been working with your local leaders to ensure your church is represented in the plans.

If not, it is not too late to get involved. As religious institutions, we are often hesitant to get into politics and that is not what I am advocating for. However, once officials are elected, they are your representatives and you want to be sure they are keeping you informed of what is happening in your city and county. You want to be sure that the budgets, laws, and ordinances that are being considered and passed will not disproportionately affect your members. Members of your church should plan to regularly attend city/county meetings, school board meetings, and participate in public planning sessions to gain an understanding of the plans for your area.

You should also consider hosting a quarterly forum for members of the community to hear from elected officials. To be fair, invite all of the officials who represent your area and allow an allotted time for each of them to speak and answer questions. If there are hot topics, allow extra time and be sure to have a strategy for crowd control to keep the conversation productive. This strategy can help the community to see your church as a resource as well as to demonstrate your influence to the elected officials.

Additionally, consult an attorney and accountant about establishing a Community Development Corporation if you do not already have one. If you have one, take some time to review your strategic plan to determine how it aligns with the city/county projects. In some cases, there may be grant funds available for you to purchase property or to provide services for your community. Having a relationship with your elected officials will put you in the position to receive that type of information.

Exercise:

Who in your congregation already has relationships with local elected officials?

How well is the congregation doing with maintaining awareness about the issues in your community?

What are some of the issues in your community that need to be addressed?

Who are the ideal persons in your congregation and community to serve on the Board of Directors for your CDC?

About CDC's

Community Development Corporations (CDCs) are nonprofit, community-based organizations focused on revitalizing the areas in which they are located, typically low-income, underserved neighborhoods that have experienced significant disinvestment. While they are most commonly celebrated for developing affordable housing, they are usually involved in a range of initiatives critical to community health such as economic development, sanitation, streetscaping, and neighborhood planning projects, and oftentimes even provide education and social services to neighborhood residents.

CDCs play a critical role in building community wealth for several key reasons:

- They anchor capital in communities by developing residential and commercial property, ranging from affordable housing to shopping centers and even businesses.
- At least one-third of a CDC's board is typically composed of community residents, allowing for the possibility of direct, grass-roots participation in decision-making.
- CDCs' work to enhance community conditions oftentimes involves neighborhood organizing, a process critical for empowering residents and gaining political power.

Source: https://community-wealth.org/strategies/panel/cdcs/index.html

Political Engagement

Goal:

OPPORTUNITIES	THREATS

Action Items

Immediate (within 6 months)
Short Term (within one year)
Long Term (within 3-5 years)

Notes:

Make Technological Upgrades

Although many churches have been slow to embrace technology as a ministry, it is imperative that you are strategic when deciding to utilize technology. Sometimes your use of technology can be more of a turn off for prospective visitors than a recruiting tool.

For example:

- Social media posts with grammatical errors lead to the assumption that your congregation is not educated or is careless about what you are sharing

- Photographs of empty congregations – most people don't want to visit or join what looks like a dead church, if you don't have good angles, don't post pictures

- Bad graphics – there are too many low-cost methods of creating flyers and marketing materials for you to post bad graphics, it signals that you are aging congregation which isn't bad if you are trying to attract other aging members

- Low-quality videos – If your viewers can not clearly hear and see what is happening, they will not stay tuned in

- Ugly and incomplete websites – it can be tempting to design your site yourself or to opt for a free site but visitors quickly navigate away from sites that are not providing relevant content, that are not optimized for mobile viewing, and that have sample text in spaces where there should be content about your ministry

- Inactive social media profiles – if you are not using the profile, consider deactivating it until you are ready; otherwise, it looks like you are not active and engaging with your community

Don't be discouraged. Here are some strategies to effectively utilize technology (social media will be addressed in the marketing plan section) in your ministry.

- ✓ AV (audio/video) within the church. Before you begin broadcasting to the world, invest in a good audio/video system for your sanctuary and fellowship hall. Make sure the people within your four walls can clearly hear what is being said. Having screens in the sanctuary is not necessary for every congregation but having one in the fellowship space for meetings is very helpful.
- ✓ Video conferencing for meetings. People are busy and cannot always attend meetings at the church. Be selective about which meetings need to be held in person and which can be conducted using a video conferencing platform. This can not only save time traveling but can also get more people involved.
- ✓ HD web camera. If you are planning to stream your services, invest in a stationary high definition web camera. They range in price but can have a great impact on the experience of those viewing your service. Using smartphones can be convenient but often catch the noise of persons around whoever is holding the phone and can also be unsteady if the holder moves around. Alternatively, you can record the sermons using a voice memo and post to an audio hosting platform until you are ready for video streaming.

Exercise:

Consult with an audio/video company to develop a plan for the ultimate experience. Start small or based on your budget and grow as your congregation grows. This is another area that can create excitement among the membership as they see the advancements.

Technology

Goal:

STRENGTHS	WEAKNESSES

Action Items

Immediate (within 6 months)
Short Term (within one year)
Long Term (within 3-5 years)

Notes:

Develop a Marketing Plan

Now that you have done most of the hard work, it is time to package it together in a way that will be attractive to the congregation and community. In many instances, consultants will have you to begin with a mission and vision statement but I like to save that for last because if you will reflect back to Page 5, some of the thoughts that you had about your church's strengths, weaknesses, opportunities, and threats may not still be a priority after our exercises. Imagine if you had spent time missioning and visioning without having contemplated the actual needs of the people you intend to serve. Too often we want to give people what we want them to have without considering to their needs.

Now that you have that information, review your mission statement and vision statement to ensure they still reflect the goals that you are setting.

Writing a mission statement
Your mission statement is used to describe why your church exists. Although all churches should exist to save the souls of humanity, your mission statement should be one sentence that succinctly describes how your church will carry out that mission.

Writing a vision statement
Your vision statement is an aspirational statement about where you see yourself in the future. Consider five adjectives that describe the future of the church and create two-three sentences using those words.

Next, let's focus on your marketing plan. You should have already amassed some of this information in the previous sections and now we will work to pull it together.

1. Demographics – currently you have two demographics to work with. You have the members within your congregation for internal marketing and

communication and the community outside of the church that you want to connect with. What are the needs of the members in each demographic and how will you meet those needs? **(What are you offering?)**

2. Target Market – for each ministry/program, you will have a target market. Is it for children, youth, young adults, adults, or mature adults? **(Who are you speaking to?)**

3. Positioning - Once you determine who you are talking to, you will not only be able to figure out what to say but also how to say it and where to share it. My favorite example to use is the cell phone. Cell phones are used by toddlers to senior saints, however, the marketing for each group is different. Same message (buy me!!) but different graphics, color schemes, placement, etc. Knowing your target market also helps you to figure out which marketing tool is best suited to reach that segment. Always ask where they spend their time and where they get information. That's where you want to be. **(Where are you sharing it?)**

4. Competition – who else is operating in this space? What other churches are in the area? What other organizations are serving the community? You can't kill off the competition but you can understand their strengths and weaknesses as well as your own to identify areas to work together by pairing one of your weaknesses with one of their strengths and vice versa. Your competitive advantage should be the relationships that you are building with your members. You can't stop them from going to other churches or not going to church at all but by building healthy relationships with them, you can encourage them to participate in the work that your church is doing. **(Why you?)**

5. Strategy – in the wrap-up, you will begin to consolidate and prioritize your projects. Once you know what you're doing, who are you doing it for,

who you are doing it with, and where you need to share; you have begun to develop a marketing strategy. **(How to implement?)**

6. Budget – there are a lot of free marketing tools but prepare to invest in your marketing because it will be seen in spaces that you may never enter. In a competitive environment, people are judging you based on the content that you share so make sure you are putting your best virtual face forward. Start small and grow. **(Where to start?)**

Finally, let's discuss some marketing tools. We will only address the basic tools to get you started. This is by no means an exhaustive list. Whatever tools you use, make sure they align with your marketing plan – stay on message and focus each campaign on your target market (you may have to create multiple pieces for one event if you're speaking to different targets).

➢ Website – your first stop should be having a website created. Many people choose social media because it is free, however, the algorithms of most platforms prevent all of your members from seeing your content. Train your members to visit your website for information about upcoming events and announcements and to use social media to share relevant information. You cannot control whether a social media platform shuts down tomorrow but you control the content on your website. A basic website should, at least, have

- information about your church, pastor, and ministries
- a contact page with a map to your location and a form for questions
- an event calendar
- a block for enewsletter signups
- a link for online donations
- a page for first time visitors

- Email marketing allows you to communicate directly with your lists. Always get permission before adding people to your list and consider segmenting your lists based on interests/ministries, age groups, class leaders, and membership status. This will allow you to easily send targeted messages.

- One sheets – on one side you should have basic information about the church and your ministries and an event listing on the other side. Keep it simple - who, what, when, where. Don't try to share everything. People don't read a lot of text. Refer them to your website for more details.

- Local media – don't forget that some people still get their news through traditional media such as newspapers and radio, most newspapers allow you to post events at little to no charge while radio stations may offer a package rate for ad bundles (consider promoting your community events instead of worship services and using secular stations instead of gospel)

- Press releases – when hosting newsworthy community events, invite the local media and submit a press release. Be sure to research templates for press releases so that they don't read like promotions or advertisements for your event because those will not be published

- Letters to the editor – when important events occur in your community, consider sending a letter to the editor of your local newspaper, these are often published online as well as in print

- Surveys – create comment cards that ask one question that will be beneficial to your ministry and requires them to provide their contact information so that you can stay in touch

- Social media – depending on the size of your team choose one to two platforms that you can post on at least once per day

- Direct mail – perhaps one of the more expensive strategies, it is often used to send postcard-sized mailers to homes within the zip code of the church to invite them to events at the church, if your budget allows, consider sending quarterly

Marketing

Goal:

STRENGTHS	WEAKNESSES

Action Items

Immediate (within 6 months)

Short Term (within one year)

Long Term (within 3-5 years)

Notes:

Wrap Up

You can do everything but you can't do everything at once. As you review your projects, use the next pages to list all of the immediate, short term and long-term action items on the next page. Begin to think of how much each action item will cost, who will be responsible, and set deadlines for their completion. Your immediate projects should be firm action items that you know need to be changed right now and you have the resources to make the adjustments. The short-term projects may be a little more fluid because they can change as you begin to experience organic growth. Revisit the list quarterly to see what adjustments need to be made. As you complete a project, consider adding another from your list. The long-term items are more aspirational and will require more human and financial resources. They will often require substantial growth for you to achieve them and they will be the most fluid. Review them quarterly also to ensure you are working toward them or to determine if they need to be changed. You may even surprise yourself with your hard work and find that you are completing your projects more quickly than planned.

It can be tempting to feel overwhelmed with all of the things that you realize you need to do to begin growing your church but remember to keep God first. Pray for God to help you discern how, when, and where He wants you to move but don't get stuck in prayer mode. Begin with the immediate items which should be easy wins for the congregation. When people begin to see change, they get excited. Some will be curious and will only come to see what's going on but that's ok. Make sure they are welcomed with open arms. Others will be skeptical and will feel certain that this won't work. Welcome them with open arms also.

If you have any questions or want to book me to present to your congregation or church group, contact me at info@WomackCG.com or search for me on any social media platforms using @LaKeshaWomack

Thank you for inviting me along this journey!

Immediate – within 6 months

Category	Action Item	Budget	Who is Responsible	Deadline
Rethinking Church		$		
Discipleship Training		$		
Class Leaders		$		
Demographics		$		
Infrastructure		$		
Evangelism		$		
Partnerships		$		
Political Engagement		$		
Technology		$		
Marketing		$		

Notes:

Short Term – within one year

Category	Action Item	Budget	Who is Responsible	Deadline
Rethinking Church		$		
Discipleship Training		$		
Class Leaders		$		
Demographics		$		
Infrastructure		$		
Evangelism		$		
Partnerships		$		
Political Engagement		$		
Technology		$		
Marketing		$		

Notes:

Long Term – 3-5 years

Category	Action Item	Budget	Who is Responsible	Deadline
Rethinking Church		$		
Discipleship Training		$		
Class Leaders		$		
Demographics		$		
Infrastructure		$		
Evangelism		$		
Partnerships		$		
Political Engagement		$		
Technology		$		
Marketing		$		

Notes:

Appendix: Abraham Maslow's Hierarchy of Needs

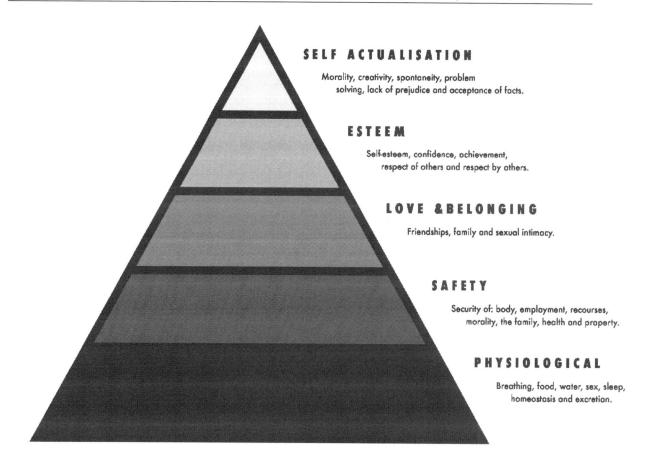

Source: https://miro.medium.com/max/3200/1*SHCMbvDHWXBiCulwzjs9bA.png